Original title:
After the Storm

Copyright © 2024 Swan Charm
All rights reserved.

Author: Liisi Lendorav
ISBN HARDBACK: 978-9916-79-264-3
ISBN PAPERBACK: 978-9916-79-265-0
ISBN EBOOK: 978-9916-79-266-7

Nature's Benediction

In the whispering woods, grace unfolds,
Each leaf a testament, in silence it holds.
Morning dew dances on fragrant blooms,
A perfect creation, where beauty consumes.

The river sings softly, a sacred hymn,
Reflecting the heavens, its edges brim.
Mountains bow low to the sky's embrace,
Nature's benediction, a holy place.

The Sanctuary of Solitude

In quiet corners, the spirit finds peace,
A sanctuary formed, where troubles cease.
Whispers of wisdom in stillness reside,
God's gentle presence, our hearts open wide.

Among towering trees, shadows dance light,
The warmth of the sun, a promise so bright.
In solitude, purpose like rivers flows,
In this sacred space, the spirit grows.

Hymn of the Rejuvenated Land

From ashes of winter, spring rises anew,
Life's vibrant palette, a heavenly view.
Flowers awaken, painting the fields,
The hymn of the land, a promise revealed.

Birds lift their voices, echoing praise,
Mountains and valleys in chorus they raise.
The earth in its bounty, a miracle grand,
In the cycle of life, we forever stand.

Baptism from Above

Raindrops descend, a celestial grace,
Each droplet a gift, cleansing the place.
With every shower, the earth is reborn,
Baptism from above, new life in the morn.

Streams swell with vigor, a dance of delight,
In puddles and lakes, reflections of light.
The world lifts its voice, in harmony call,
A sacred baptism, embracing us all.

Celestial Horizons

In the silence of dawn's grace,
Angels sing with soft embrace,
The stars awake to lift the day,
Guiding souls along the way.

Infinity calls from above,
With a promise of endless love,
Each heartbeat a sacred song,
Together we shall strive along.

Through valleys of faith we tread,
In the light where shadows fled,
Hope ignites in hearts so pure,
In the Savior, we find our cure.

Celestial paths our spirits roam,
Led by whispers that feel like home,
Embracing peace amidst the strife,
A tapestry woven with eternal life.

To the heavens, our eyes ascend,
In this journey, we shall mend,
Trusting in the divine plan,
Hand in hand, we'll understand.

A Rebirth in Spirits

In the hush of twilight's glow,
New beginnings start to flow,
Forgiveness whispered on the breeze,
Softening hearts, bringing ease.

From ashes rises sacred fire,
With each spark, we build our choir,
Voices lift in joyous praise,
Rebirth shines in myriad ways.

The spirit's journey knows no end,
Through trials, we shall transcend,
Faith like rivers flowing free,
Embracing all that's meant to be.

In unity, our souls ignite,
Guided by His holy light,
Together we shall seek and find,
The love that binds all humankind.

A dance of grace upon the earth,
Each moment, a sacred birth,
In every heart, His spirit glows,
In the stillness, true life grows.

The Light's Journey Home

In the darkness, light arrives,
A beacon where our spirit thrives,
Stepping boldly toward the dawn,
In His presence, fear is gone.

With every breath, we rise anew,
Truth reflected in all we do,
Casting shadows, doubts, and fear,
In His embrace, we draw near.

Traveling paths of joy and grace,
Finding hope in every place,
Hearts united, voices clear,
A chorus of faith, love, and cheer.

Through the valleys, through the storm,
Our souls transformed, our spirits warm,
Each step a testament of faith,
In His light, we find our place.

The journey home begins with trust,
In His promises, we can adjust,
With every heartbeat, prayers take flight,
Guided always by the light.

Waters of Purity Flow

From mountain springs to rivers wide,
Grace cascades like ocean tide,
Each drop a blessing to behold,
In the waters, truth unfolds.

With every stream that gently winds,
The essence of love entwines,
Cleansing sorrows, washing pain,
In His mercy, hope remains.

Bathe in purity, find your peace,
In His presence, all fears cease,
Hearts awaken, spirits soar,
As we drink from the sacred shore.

The waters whisper ancient tales,
Of faith and love that never fails,
Flowing through the landscape of souls,
Unifying the broken, making whole.

In the depths, His spirit glows,
A river of grace eternally flows,
Dive deep, let your spirit rise,
In these waters, the heart replies.

The Pathway to Grace

In the quiet whispers of dawn,
Faith beckons from shadows deep.
Steps echo where spirits have gone,
Guiding hearts that long to leap.

With each prayer, the burden lifts,
Hope blooms in the fertile soul.
Grace pours down like gentle gifts,
Filling voids and making whole.

Through trials where tempests rage,
We find peace in the storm's embrace.
The turning of a holy page,
Reveals love, our sacred space.

In the gardens of the divine,
Every flower sings of light.
Paths converging, hearts align,
In unity, we take flight.

So walk this way, with eyes aglow,
Let love's anthem be your song.
For on this road, we come to know,
In grace, we finally belong.

A Remnant's Reverie

In the stillness of the night,
Stars whisper ancient tales.
Remnants of faith take flight,
On the wind, the spirit sails.

Echoes of prayers long past,
Dance upon the moonlit sea.
A light that forever casts,
Radiance on memories free.

With hearts open, we reflect,
On journeys that shaped our soul.
Each step taken, we connect,
To the Source that makes us whole.

In reverie, we find the grace,
Of those who walked the sacred ground.
In every heartbeat, love's embrace,
A remnant's song— forever found.

For in the still, we remember,
The path forged by those before.
Their flames ignite our own ember,
Together, forevermore.

Transcendence in Stillness

In quietude, we seek the light,
Moments pause, our spirits soar.
Through stillness, we glimpse the bright,
Transcendence opens every door.

Beneath the weight of worldly care,
Peace beckons from beyond the veil.
In silence, souls lay bare,
And hearts unleash a hopeful trail.

With every breath, a prayer ascends,
Whispers of love in sacred time.
As night to day, the soul transcends,
In the rhythm of the divine rhyme.

Fractured thoughts now find their place,
In the calm of a holy sphere.
Together we embrace that grace,
Knowing we are always near.

To linger in this hallowed calm,
Where essence flows and wisdom sings.
In stillness, we discover balm,
And the truth that stillness brings.

In Search of the Celestial

Across the heavens, visions gleam,
Hearts wander on wings of prayer.
In shadows deep, we chase a dream,
Of realms untouched, beyond compare.

Through valleys low and mountains high,
The weary seek what is divine.
With outstretched arms to the sky,
In search of the eternal sign.

Each star a beacon, hope reborn,
As galaxies reveal their grace.
In cosmic dance, our spirits sworn,
To find our place in sacred space.

The cosmos hums a gentle tune,
Inviting all to join the flight.
In the embrace of sun and moon,
We glimpse the beauty of the light.

So let us wander, bold and free,
In search of truth, we lift our gaze.
For in the celestial we see,
The love that bridges all our ways.

Forgiveness in the Form of Rain

The clouds gather, a gentle sigh,
In the hush of the evening sky.
Each drop a whisper from above,
Cleansing hearts with endless love.

Let go of burdens, let them flow,
Here in the rain, our spirits grow.
Flowing like rivers, pure and bright,
Forgiveness shines in soft twilight.

Through puddles formed, we see the light,
Mirroring grace, dispelling night.
In nature's rhythm, we unite,
Healing rains renew our sight.

So lift your hands, embrace the grace,
Let forgiveness find its place.
Each moment cherished, souls reborn,
In the gentle rain, we'll be adorned.

The Book of Winds and Waves

Upon the sea, the winds do sigh,
A tale of faith, beneath the sky.
Every wave, a verse of prayer,
Whispering truths in salty air.

The storms may come, but fear not stray,
Trust in the path, come what may.
In every crest and every trough,
Hear the promise, ever soft.

Lessons learned through tempest's roar,
Bring us closer to the shore.
A lighthouse stands, steadfast and bright,
Guiding hearts through endless night.

So in this book of winds and tides,
Let faith be where our hope abides.
In harmony with sea and sky,
We find our strength, we learn to fly.

Songs from the Refreshed Heart

In quiet corners, the heart sings,
Of grace, of love, and sacred things.
With every beat, a melody,
Refreshed by hope eternally.

The chorus rises, soft and sweet,
In gentle rhythms, spirits meet.
A symphony of joy reborn,
In every dawn, a new day's morn.

Each note a prayer, each verse a blessing,
In our souls, the light releasing.
Together in this sacred art,
We weave the songs from the heart.

So let us gather, hand in hand,
In unity, we understand.
The songs of peace, they rise and soar,
Binding us forevermore.

Resounding Praise in the Stillness

In the quiet hour, praises rise,
Carried forth to heavenly skies.
In stillness found, our hearts align,
With whispers soft, a sacred sign.

The moonlight filters through the trees,
A symphony upon the breeze.
Every shadow holds a prayer,
Resounding joy fills the air.

In tranquil moments, grace abounds,
In silent awe, the spirit sounds.
With every breath, a hymn we share,
In the stillness, God is there.

Let every soul send forth a song,
In unity, where we belong.
With grateful hearts and voices raised,
Together we resound in praise.

Wisdom in the Winds

In whispers of the breeze we find,
The ancient truths that time unwinds.
Each rustle speaks of journeys past,
A sacred dance that ever lasts.

The trees bow low, their secrets shared,
In silent prayers, they are prepared.
With every gust, a voice divine,
Guiding hearts to the sacred line.

A symphony of nature's grace,
In every shadow, light's embrace.
The winds carry our hopes and fears,
Their gentle touch, the passage of years.

The soaring eagle, wise and proud,
In heights above, he speaks so loud.
With each flight through the azure sky,
He teaches us to wonder why.

So listen close, the winds will tell,
Of love and lessons, all is well.
In nature's breath, we find our way,
To wisdom bright as break of day.

The Atonement of Nature

In fields of gold where daisies bloom,
There lies a grace that lifts the gloom.
Each petal soft, a promise made,
Of healing rains that will cascade.

The mountains rise with silent might,
Guardians of day and cloak of night.
Their rugged forms, a path to tread,
In search of truths that lie ahead.

The rivers flow with gentle song,
Their currents strong, yet never wrong.
They carve the land with tender care,
A testimony, woven rare.

The storms will come, yet so they go,
In every clash, the seeds we sow.
The earth will tremble, then restore,
A love that binds forevermore.

In twilight's glow, the peace descends,
Nature's cycle, it never bends.
In every loss, a chance to gain,
Redemption born from nature's pain.

A Divine Dialogue

In silent prayer, we seek the light,
A conversation through the night.
With every breath, our spirits rise,
In whispered words, the heart replies.

The stars above, like candles bright,
Illuminate our quest for sight.
Their twinkling speaks of dreams so high,
A dialogue between earth and sky.

In moments still, the soul can hear,
The echo of the love so near.
Each heartbeat a reminder clear,
That in the dark, the light is dear.

Through trials faced and paths unknown,
In faith we walk, not alone.
For in each struggle, whispers say,
A sacred bond will guide the way.

So let us talk, with spirits bold,
In every story, truth unfolds.
A divine exchange of grace and fear,
In every moment, love is near.

Beneath the Canvas of Hope

Beneath the sky, a tapestry,
Of colors bright, a sight to see.
Each hue a dream that soars and swirls,
A canvas rich, where hope unfurls.

The sunrise paints the world anew,
With golden rays and morning dew.
In every dawn, a promise grows,
A whisper of what life bestows.

The sunset brings a soft goodbye,
As stars emerge in evening's sigh.
A moment's pause, a time to rest,
In every breath, we are so blessed.

The moon above, a guiding light,
In darkest hours, she shines so bright.
Her silver beams on paths we roam,
A gentle touch that leads us home.

So let us cherish every hue,
In life's great art, both old and new.
For beneath the heavens wide and clear,
Hope thrives eternal, always near.

The Divine Resurgence

In shadows deep, the spirits rise,
Awakening hope beneath the skies.
With faith ablaze, we seek the light,
From ashes born, our souls take flight.

To every heart that feels alone,
The whispers guide us toward the throne.
In sacred songs, our voices blend,
A symphony that never ends.

With every step upon this ground,
The sacred path of grace is found.
Emerging strong from trials faced,
In holy love, we are embraced.

A tapestry of tears and dreams,
Woven tight with silver beams.
As dawn unfolds, new life will spring,
In every breath, our praises sing.

The flame of truth, it ever glows,
Through trials fierce, our spirit flows.
In unity, we rise anew,
The divine mercy guiding through.

Light Amidst the Ruins

Through broken walls, the daylight breaks,
A tender touch, each heart it wakes.
In desolation's tight embrace,
The light of hope reveals its grace.

From shattered dreams, new visions form,
In chaos lies a sacred norm.
With every bruise, a story told,
Of strength and love, a truth of old.

When shadows cling and doubts arise,
The light appears in gentle sighs.
With lifted hands, we seek the way,
To brighter dawns, to brighter day.

In ruins deep, our spirits soar,
Through faith's resilience, we restore.
The broken past, a path we claim,
In every soul, ignites a flame.

Though storms may rage and darkness loom,
We find our shelter, we find our room.
In unity we stand, we thrive,
In love's embrace, we come alive.

The Touch of the Almighty

In stillness found, the Spirit flows,
A gentle breeze, the heart it knows.
With every breath, a touch divine,
Awakening love, forever mine.

Through trials faced, through tears we shed,
The hand of grace, our spirit led.
In whispered prayers, we seek the fate,
Of boundless love, we elevate.

Upon the mount, where silence reigns,
The touch of God, it eases pains.
In valleys low, His voice is clear,
A guiding light that draws us near.

With every heartbeat, peace unfolds,
In sacred tales, the truth retold.
The touch of the Almighty brings,
A harmony in all things sings.

As rivers flow and seasons change,
His presence lingers, never strange.
In every moment, we are blessed,
With heaven's love, our hearts at rest.

Clover and Clouds in Communion

In fields of clover, softness grows,
Beneath the clouds, the spirit knows.
A dance of nature, hand in hand,
In sacred rhythms, we will stand.

Each petal speaks of grace bestowed,
In unity, the heart's abode.
Through gentle rains, a promise made,
In every drop, our fears will fade.

When skies are grey and shadows loom,
We find the light that chases gloom.
With every bloom, a sacred place,
In clover's touch, we find His grace.

The whispers of the wind declare,
Connection deep, beyond compare.
As clouds embrace the golden sun,
In unity, we are all one.

In nature's arms, we rest and pray,
Each moment counts, each breath, a way.
Clover and clouds, our hearts as one,
In divine love, our journey's begun.

Silence Between the Thunder

In the stillness after the storm,
He whispers soft to weary hearts,
A calm that shields from raging harm,
In silence grace and hope imparts.

When lightning strikes and fears arise,
Look beyond the blinding light,
For there within that chaos lies,
A peace, a path to truth and right.

The thunder rolls, yet faith remains,
Unshaken by the deafening sound,
A quiet trust that breaks the chains,
In the heart where love is found.

Amidst the shouts and cries of night,
Stillness lays its gentle claim,
In every moment, pure delight,
The whisper calls us by His name.

Breaking of the Chains

From shadows deep, the lost are found,
With every bond that breaks away,
The light of dawn can now resound,
In freedom's arms, our spirits sway.

Chains of despair, they fall and shatter,
Forged in fear, now turned to dust,
With every step, our hearts grow fatter,
In love's embrace, we learn to trust.

Through trials faced, a strength appears,
A joy ignited from the pain,
With every tear and silent fear,
A bitter loss now blooms again.

Together we rise, hand in hand,
United voices, hearts aflame,
For in His love, we take a stand,
No longer bound, we claim His name.

Ascending from Ashes

From ruins wrought by grief and sorrow,
New life emerges, fierce and bright,
With each dawn, a brand new tomorrow,
We rise from ashes, into light.

The fire may burn, but it transforms,
A sacred alchemy of grace,
In every wound, a spirit warms,
Breathing life into our space.

Hope unfurls like wings anew,
From darkest nights, we find our flight,
In trials faced, our strength will brew,
We soar beyond the starry night.

With faith that guides, we choose to stand,
Each step a promise, bold and true,
In His embrace, we find our land,
A legacy of love imbues.

The Dawn of Redemption

When night is long and shadows creep,
A promise stirs, igniting hope,
In darkest hours, we wake from sleep,
To find the way, we learn to cope.

Redemption's light breaks through the veil,
A gentle hand to lift the meek,
In every trial, our spirits sail,
Towards tomorrow's brighter peak.

With hearts renewed, we rise again,
Awakening to grace's song,
In love's embrace, we make amends,
And find where we truly belong.

The dawn unfolds, a canvas bright,
With colors drawn from tears now dried,
In every soul, a spark of light,
Together, born of love, we ride.

A Testament Written in Sky

Beneath the arch of heaven's glow,
Words of wisdom softly flow.
Stars like sparks of faith ignite,
Guiding souls through darkest night.

Clouds bear witness to our dreams,
Carved in air, as hope redeems.
Each sunset paints a sacred line,
A testament, eternally divine.

With every dawn, a promise born,
Of grace and love in a world worn.
The heavens whisper, clear and bright,
A canvas vast, reflecting light.

In silence, prayers take their flight,
Carried forth on winds of light.
The sky becomes our sacred tome,
In its embrace, we find our home.

When Thunder Becomes a Whisper

In storms where chaos reigns supreme,
A voice of peace, a gentle dream.
When thunder roars, our hearts may quake,
Yet in the hush, the world will wake.

Raindrops fall as softest sighs,
Life's rhythm set beneath dark skies.
Each flash of light, a fleeting grace,
Telling tales of our sacred space.

In nature's orchestra, we find,
A harmony that lifts the blind.
When silence speaks, the spirit flows,
In whispered truths, the heart still knows.

With every clash, a lesson learned,
In stillness waits what's truly yearned.
For when storms pass and calm returns,
The dance of faith within us burns.

Serenity Found in Ruins

Among the stones where shadows dwell,
A story hidden, yet to tell.
In broken walls, a heart's deep sigh,
Echoes of laughter still float by.

Nature weaves through cracks of time,
In silent grace, the vines will climb.
Each step through history's embrace,
Reveals a sacred, timeless place.

Amidst the dust of what once was,
We find the light without a cause.
In every ruin, love remains,
A bond unbroken, beyond chains.

With every heartbeat, we reclaim,
The sacred echoes of His name.
Serenity blooms where hope is sown,
In the whispers of the unknown.

Trees with Arms Open Wide

In ancient woods, where spirits dwell,
The trees stand tall, their tales to tell.
With arms outstretched, they greet the sun,
In every leaf, the love's begun.

Roots entwined in earth's embrace,
A shelter found in nature's grace.
Each branch a prayer, each rustle song,
In the forest's heart, we all belong.

Seasons change, yet still they stand,
Guardians of this sacred land.
Their whispers soft, like sacred vows,
In harmony, they teach us how.

As shadows dance in golden light,
A sacred balm for every plight.
In gathering storms, they sway and bend,
But in their strength, we find our mend.

Echoes of Divine Love

In silence, whispers of grace,
Hearts lifted in embrace.
Heaven's light ignites the soul,
Binding us, making us whole.

Every tear, a sacred thread,
In love's tapestry, we're led.
Through trials, His voice we hear,
A melody, drawing us near.

The stars proclaim His gentle song,
In unity, we learn to belong.
With open arms, we share the way,
Guided by love, come what may.

In deeds of kindness, hope prevails,
As faith unfurls, and doubt pales.
Together we walk, hand in hand,
In this beautiful promised land.

Echoes of grace in each heartbeat,
In the divine, our lives complete.
With every prayer, we sow the seeds,
Of endless love that truly leads.

The Pathway to Salvation

Upon the road, shadows fade,
In faith and trust, we are laid.
With every step, burdens decrease,
In His presence, we find peace.

The narrow gate, where souls unite,
In His arms, we find true light.
Whispers guide us through the night,
With every prayer, we seek the right.

Temptations rise, yet hearts remain,
In storms of doubt, we find our gain.
Together as one, we shall embrace,
A journey marked by endless grace.

Through valleys deep and mountains tall,
Together we rise, together we fall.
In hope's embrace, our spirits soar,
Together upwards, forevermore.

The pathway to salvation clear,
In love's reflection, we persevere.
With every heartbeat, souls entwine,
In this sacred truth, we shall shine.

Unseen Hands of Compassion

Beneath the surface, love extends,
Unseen hands where kindness bends.
In quiet moments, grace will flow,
In gentle acts, His mercy grows.

We gather strength from every care,
In shared burdens, hearts laid bare.
With open hearts, we serve with grace,
In every smile, His warm embrace.

Through suffering, we find our way,
In love's reflection, night turns to day.
We plant the seeds of hope so bright,
With each touch, we share His light.

In darkness, let compassion rise,
With every hope, our spirits fly.
Together we face the trials ahead,
In love's communion, darkness fled.

Unseen hands weave the fabric tight,
Binding us in endless light.
With every heartbeat intertwined,
In love's embrace, we're all aligned.

Beneath the Scattered Leaves

Beneath the scattered leaves we tread,
In nature's grace, our spirits spread.
The whispers of the ancient trees,
Invite our souls to find the ease.

In every rustle, life unfolds,
A tapestry of stories told.
In every shadow, light will break,
With every sigh, His heart we make.

The autumn's chill, a call to pray,
In solemn moments, find the way.
With gratitude, we gather near,
In every heartbeat, He draws near.

Through seasons' change, our faith remains,
In love's embrace, we bear the pains.
Each fallen leaf, a lesson learned,
In nature's cycle, hearts discerned.

Beneath the scattered leaves, we grow,
In constant grace, our spirits flow.
With every breath, we feel the sway,
Of His endless love, day by day.

Triumph of the Spirit

In quiet faith the spirit soars,
Rising above with gentle roars.
In trials faced, we find our might,
Guided by love, we share the light.

Through shadows deep, the hope we cling,
In every heart, a song to sing.
With every step, we rise anew,
In grace bestowed, our path is true.

The trials faced, a sculptor's hand,
Chiseling strength as we take a stand.
Our spirits intertwined in prayer,
A bond unbroken, forever rare.

With eyes uplifted, we shall see,
The greater path, our destiny.
In unity, our voices blend,
With every heartbeat, love transcends.

In triumph found, we walk as one,
Embracing light, our work begun.
For in the spirit, we shall rise,
To meet the dawn beyond the skies.

Ways of the Blessed

On paths of grace, the blessed walk,
In whispered prayers, our spirits talk.
With every step, we seek to know,
The love that flows, the seed we sow.

With open hearts, we share our dreams,
In joy and sorrow, love redeems.
Together strong, we rise above,
Reflecting faith, and boundless love.

In every kindness, blessings grow,
A gentle hand, a heart aglow.
With faith as light, our way is clear,
In stillness found, we draw Him near.

Through stormy seas, our souls shall steer,
In guiding stars, we find no fear.
With voices raised, we sing as one,
In every deed, His will be done.

The ways of blessed weave stories bright,
In unity, we shine in light.
With steadfast hearts, we rise and stand,
In His embrace, we find our land.

Embracing Celestial Auras

Beneath the heavens, souls entwine,
In radiant grace, the light divine.
With every breath, we feel the flow,
Of sacred dreams, in colors glow.

In whispers soft, the cosmos sings,
In filigreed light, the love it brings.
Through fields of stars, we find our way,
Embracing night, and welcoming day.

In silence deep, the spirit knows,
Awakening strength in quiet rows.
With hearts aligned, we dance in trance,
In celestial love, we sing, we prance.

With every pulse, the universe breathes,
In harmony, the heart believes.
In knowing peace, we seek to soar,
United souls, forevermore.

In dreams we weave, a tapestry bright,
Reflecting love in purest light.
Together bound, in this embrace,
Celestial auras, our sacred space.

Blossoms of the Renewed

From ashes rise, new blossoms bloom,
In fragrant gardens, dispelling gloom.
Each petal soft, a tale of grace,
In every heart, we find our place.

Through trials faced, the roots go deep,
In faith awakened, our promises keep.
With every dawn, a chance to grow,
Embracing light, our spirits glow.

In unity, our voices blend,
Through storms we face, our hearts transcend.
With hope as fuel, we journey on,
In love renewed, we greet the dawn.

With open arms, we share the love,
Embracing blessings from above.
The blossoms shine in colors bright,
A testament to faith's pure light.

In every soul, a journey starts,
A seed of joy within our hearts.
So let us bloom, in grace anew,
Blossoms of hope, forever true.

Resounding Hallelujahs

In morning light, our voices rise,
With grateful hearts, we lift our cries.
The angels join in sacred song,
A chorus sweet, where all belong.

With every breath, the praises flow,
In unity, our spirits grow.
Through trials faced, we find our way,
With faith in each and every day.

The stars above, they shine so bright,
A testament to love's own light.
In silence deep, we hear the call,
The resounding hallelujahs fall.

From mountains high to valleys low,
The reverence in our hearts we sow.
In every joy, and every tear,
We find the grace that draws us near.

O Lord, we sing, our souls aflame,
In endless praise, we bless your name.
With every note, our spirits soar,
In harmony, forevermore.

The Hand That Guides Us

In shadows deep, when fears arise,
A gentle hand wipes tears from eyes.
With steady love, it holds us tight,
Through stormy seas and darkest night.

When paths are unclear and hope seems lost,
We find our strength, despite the cost.
The hand that guides us, firm and true,
Leads us forth to all that's new.

With every step, through joy and pain,
We trust the hand that bears our strain.
In whispered prayers, our souls align,
With grace divine, we shall soon shine.

When burdens weigh upon the heart,
A guiding touch plays its sweet part.
We walk by faith, not by our sight,
Forever led by love's pure light.

O Lord, in you, our spirits thrive,
With every heartbeat, we are alive.
In every moment, near or far,
Your guiding hand, our shining star.

Gifts of the Unseen

In quiet moments, blessings dwell,
The gifts of love, too pure to tell.
With every breath, we find the grace,
A hidden light in sacred space.

Through acts of kindness, love is shown,
A gentle touch, though not our own.
In laughter shared, and tears we spill,
The unseen gifts, they guide our will.

With each soft whisper, truth unfolds,
In stories shared, the heart consoles.
In silence held, our spirits blend,
The love divine that knows no end.

In nature's breath, the colors bright,
We see the gifts of pure delight.
In every soul, a spark ignites,
The unseen love, it takes to flight.

O Lord, we treasure what you bring,
In humble hearts, we yearn to sing.
The gifts of the unseen, so vast,
In gratitude, our souls are cast.

Sanctified Landscapes

In fields of green, where flowers bloom,
God's handiwork dispels all gloom.
The mountains rise, they touch the sky,
In sanctified lands, our spirits fly.

The rivers flow with songs of peace,
In nature's arms, our worries cease.
Each tree a whisper, each stone a prayer,
In sacred spaces, we find repair.

The sun, it sets in hues divine,
A canvas bright where spirits shine.
In twilight's glow, our hearts align,
In sanctified landscapes, love we find.

With every step on hallowed ground,
In harmony, we hear the sound.
From ocean's wave to desert's grace,
In all creation, we find His face.

O Lord, through nature, we behold,
The wonders of your love untold.
In every landscape, near or far,
Your presence true, our guiding star.

Graceful Resilience

In the quiet dawn, faith blooms bright,
A gentle whisper in the night.
Through trials faced, we rise anew,
Strength in the heart, steadfast and true.

With every tear, a lesson learned,
In the flame of love, our spirits burned.
We walk the path, though steep and wide,
Graceful resilience, our humble guide.

When shadows fall, we stand as one,
United beneath the radiant sun.
Each step we take, a sacred dance,
With every challenge, we find our chance.

In moments dark, when hope seems lost,
We gather strength, no matter the cost.
A tapestry woven with threads of gold,
Stories of courage, eternally bold.

With every heartbeat, a prayer we send,
In love's embrace, we learn to mend.
Graceful resilience, a gift we share,
In the fabric of faith, forever aware.

Chasing the Light Beyond

In the twilight glow, our spirits rise,
Chasing the light that never lies.
Through valleys low and mountains vast,
We seek the truth, our shadows cast.

With open hearts, we dare to dream,
Every whisper feels like a beam.
In the distance, a promise gleams,
Guiding us forth through sacred themes.

When storms encroach, and fears entwine,
We lift our voices, a sacred line.
Faith is the beacon cutting through night,
Chasing the light, our souls take flight.

In gentle breezes, the Spirit leads,
Planting within us the hopeful seeds.
We learn to grow through trials by fire,
Chasing the light, we rise ever higher.

As dawn awakens, our hearts align,
In unity, we find the divine.
Chasing the light, our purpose clear,
With every step, our heaven is near.

Embracing Hope's Echo

In the silence, hope softly calls,
Resonating through hallowed halls.
With every heartbeat, an echo rings,
Embracing the love that faith brings.

Through trials faced, we learn to bend,
In brokenness, we find a friend.
Holding the light in shadows cast,
Embracing hope, our prayers steadfast.

When darkness looms, and doubts take flight,
We seek the spark that ignites the night.
In whispered prayers, our spirits soar,
Embracing hope, forevermore.

With gentle hands, we weave our dreams,
In every heart, the promise gleams.
Embracing hope, we stand as one,
Illuminated by the morning sun.

In the space between despair and grace,
We find connection, a sacred place.
Embracing hope, we rise with the dawn,
In love's embrace, we are reborn.

Faith in Forgotten Corners

In forgotten corners, faith remains,
Tucked away where love sustains.
In whispers low, a prayer is sown,
Seeds of hope in every heart grown.

Through unseen trials, we search and seek,
In the quiet stillness, the humble speak.
Faith in the small, in moments unseen,
A flicker of light, forever keen.

With gentle hands, we gather the lost,
Carrying love, no matter the cost.
In the depths of night, our candles shine,
Faith in forgotten corners, divine.

When paths are weary and voices fade,
We find our strength in the prayers made.
In hidden places, our spirits thrive,
Faith in the heart, forever alive.

With every dawn, a new chance is born,
In forgotten corners, hope is worn.
Faith, like a river, finds its course,
Binding us all with an endless source.

The Psalm of the Cleansing Winds

O gentle winds, arise and blow,
Through valleys deep, where shadows grow.
With every breath, pure grace descend,
And heal the hearts that seek to mend.

Awake the soul from slumber's night,
In whispered prayers, bring forth the light.
Cleansing streams of mercy, flow,
Refresh the spirit, let love sow.

Let winds of change, like rivers, sweep,
Awakening the dreams we keep.
Through every grove and mountain high,
May hope's embrace be ever nigh.

So raise your hands, let praises soar,
In gratitude, we shall implore.
For every gust, a chance to see,
The beauty found in pure decree.

O winds of time, your song we sing,
In harmony, our hearts take wing.
With every breath, we come alive,
In cleansing winds, our souls revive.

Harmony Beyond the Chaos

In chaos' midst, a peaceful song,
A melody that sweeps along.
Through shattered dreams and torn apart,
The harmony resides in heart.

Empowered souls in darkness rise,
With faith unyielding, they are wise.
Each note a beacon shining bright,
Guiding us through the longest night.

A symphony of hope we play,
With every chord, we find the way.
Together, hand in hand we stand,
Creating peace across the land.

In every trial, the spirit hums,
Uniting us as hope becomes.
Beyond the chaos, love will reign,
In sacred bonds, we break the chain.

So let our hearts, like arrows, fly,
Unfurling dreams that touch the sky.
In harmony, we find our voice,
And in the love, we shall rejoice.

When Chaos Meets Divinity

When chaos strikes with thunderous might,
A whisper calls, a guiding light.
In trembling hearts, a spark ignites,
As souls awaken to new heights.

Divinity dances in the storm,
Embracing all in sacred form.
For every trial that tests our way,
Hope blossoms bright, come what may.

In storms of life, we find our ground,
With faith and love forever bound.
The tempest roars, but we stand still,
In trust and grace, we bend our will.

So when the world feels torn apart,
Look to the divine within your heart.
For chaos is the path we tread,
To find the peace that lies ahead.

Let every tear that falls like rain,
Be transformed into joy, not pain.
In chaos' grip, divinity flows,
A sacred truth that life bestows.

The Promise of New Dawn

At dawn's first light, a promise wakes,
With every ray, the silence breaks.
A tender hope, a brand new start,
In every soul, a beating heart.

For shadows fade with morning's grace,
As love extends its warm embrace.
With every breath, we rise anew,
To greet the day, our spirits true.

The heavens shout, the earth replies,
In unity, the spirit flies.
With every bloom, a sign appears,
The promise held for countless years.

So gather strength from fields of light,
Embrace the dawn, banish the night.
For every trial, a lesson guides,
Through every tear, a joy abides.

In trust we stand, hearts full and free,
Embracing all that's meant to be.
As dawn unfolds, our spirits raise,
In gratitude, we sing His praise.

The Journey Toward the Sun

In darkness we wander, seeking the light,
With faith as our guide, we embrace the night.
Each step is a prayer, a whisper of grace,
The sun beckons softly, our hearts start to race.

With hopes like the stars, we rise and ascend,
Through trials and shadows, our spirits shall mend.
Together we walk on this path ever bright,
The journey toward sun, our future in sight.

The dawn will break forth, illuminating all,
In the warmth of His love, we will never fall.
For in unity's strength, we find our true song,
The journey toward sun, where we all belong.

Embrace every moment, with joy in your soul,
In the heart of the tempest, we find ourselves whole.
With gratitude as armor, we never shall tire,
The journey toward sun, igniting our fire.

Let hope guide our hearts, let love be our guide,
In the arms of the dawn, we shall abide.
For every small step leads us closer to grace,
The journey toward sun, our true resting place.

Fragrance of Hope Amidst the Debris

In ruins we gather, where sorrow had spread,
Yet blooms of resilience rise up from the dead.
With whispers of courage, we lift up our eyes,
The fragrance of hope, as the ashes arise.

Amidst all despair, there's beauty in plight,
Each petal a promise, igniting the night.
Though storms may encircle, our spirits will soar,
The fragrance of hope, forever restore.

With faith intertwined like vines on a wall,
We stand in the shadows, yet hear the call.
From heartache to healing, together we weave,
The fragrance of hope, in all who believe.

In gardens of grace, let love be our seed,
For every small kindness shall flourish and lead.
Through trials and tests, we embrace what we see,
The fragrance of hope, setting our spirits free.

So gather ye souls, let harmony ring,
In the depths of despair, new life shall spring.
For from brokenness blooms the greatest decree,
The fragrance of hope, amidst the debris.

Whispers of Renewal

In silence we ponder, a world transformed,
Through gentle reflections, our hearts are warmed.
With each sacred moment, the spirit resides,
Whispers of renewal in the tides.

Time flows like water, refreshing and pure,
In valleys of stillness, we silently stir.
As seasons awaken, our spirits take flight,
Whispers of renewal, leading to light.

In shadows that linger, let dreams take their form,
Through trials and trials, we weather the storm.
With echoes of promise that rise from the dew,
Whispers of renewal, always ring true.

For every small gesture, each hand that we hold,
Is a thread in the tapestry, woven in gold.
A journey of kindness, where hearts intertwine,
Whispers of renewal, blessings divine.

So listen, dear soul, as the cosmos sings,
Of love everlasting, of infinite things.
For in every heartbeat, in joy and in pain,
Whispers of renewal, our life's sweet refrain.

The Sanctuary Awaits

In the heart of the storm, there's refuge and peace,
Where love finds a harbor, and fears find release.
A sanctuary built on the hopes we impart,
The sanctuary awaits, where we gather our heart.

With open arms welcoming all who draw near,
In shadows transformed, we vanquish the fear.
Together we thrive, in trust and in grace,
The sanctuary awaits, a warm, sacred place.

With wisdom like rivers, we flow and connect,
In moments of silence, we learn to reflect.
Hand in hand moving toward the dawn's gentle hue,
The sanctuary awaits, in all that we do.

In laughter and tears, our spirits unite,
Creating a canvas painted in light.
With love as our guide, we cherish this fate,
The sanctuary awaits, it's never too late.

So come, weary traveler, lay down your strife,
In the arms of compassion, you'll find your new life.
For in this embrace, we find what it's worth,
The sanctuary awaits, a glimpse of new birth.

Beneath the Shattered Sky

Beneath the shattered sky we stand,
In prayerful whispers, hand in hand.
With broken dreams, our hopes will rise,
A promise held in sacred ties.

The clouds may darken, storms may brew,
Yet faith abides in all we do.
From ashes, light will surely gleam,
Awakening the truest dream.

In shadows cast by doubt and fear,
We find the grace that draws us near.
Each tear we shed, a sacred sigh,
Beneath the shattered, we learn to fly.

The earth bears scars from battles fought,
In every loss, a lesson taught.
Through trials deep, we seek the way,
To turn our night into the day.

With spirits drawn to realms above,
In every heart, a seed of love.
With shattered skies, we'll build anew,
In faith's embrace, we will break through.

A Covenant of Raindrops

In each raindrop, a covenant flows,
With whispered vows, the earth bestows.
A blessing soft, a promise pure,
In nature's arms, we find our cure.

As rivers swell and mountains bow,
The sacred dance commands a vow.
In every drop, a story spun,
Of life reborn, of battles won.

When skies weep joy, when storms prevail,
In every heart, we hear the tale.
Of love awakened, deep and wide,
A covenant that we abide.

The rhythm of the rain, a hymn,
That calls us forth when hope grows dim.
Each droplet sings of peace untold,
As nature's truths begin to unfold.

From clouded skies to earth's embrace,
We find our strength in every grace.
With every storm, we shall be free,
In raindrops' bliss, we find the key.

The Light Unveiled

In darkness deep, we seek the way,
A flicker shines, dispels the gray.
The light unveiled in tender grace,
A sacred glow, our souls retrace.

With every heartbeat, truth is found,
In whispers soft, in love unbound.
The shadows speak, but light will sing,
A melody of life, our offering.

From seams of doubt, the light will break,
For every heart that dares to wake.
A guiding flame through trials vast,
A tether strong, our shadows cast.

The dawn will rise, with colors bright,
Restoring hope, igniting night.
In every soul, a spark divine,
The light revealed, our fates entwine.

In love's embrace, we are restored,
Through veils of time, with faith adored.
The light unveiled, our spirits soar,
With every step, we seek for more.

In the Wake of the Tempest

In the wake of the tempest, peace is born,
New hope arises with the dawn.
The winds may howl, the oceans roar,
Yet after storms, we find much more.

With battered sails, we chart our course,
In every challenge, a sacred force.
From chaos springs a tranquil sea,
A whispered promise we are free.

Through raging tides and shadows cast,
We hold to faith, to love steadfast.
In trials faced, our spirits gleam,
For every storm reveals a dream.

The heart once heavy learns to rise,
Transformed by tears and sacred ties.
In the wake of tempests, we discover,
A path to peace like no other.

The world restored with every breath,
In every ending, life from death.
In storms we find our strength defined,
In the wake of tempests, hearts aligned.

Harvest Under Hallowed Skies

Beneath the sun's embrace, we toil,
In fields of grace, our hands uncoil.
Each seed we sow, a prayer of peace,
In harvest time, may blessings increase.

The golden grains, they sway and dance,
In rhythm with life's sacred chance.
The bounty shared, with joy we lift,
Our hearts in thanks, a humble gift.

The earth replies, with whispered song,
In harmony where we belong.
Together we join, in faith and cheer,
Under hallowed skies, the Divine draws near.

With open hearts, we gather round,
Each laughter shared, a holy sound.
As seasons change, we find our way,
In gratefulness, we praise each day.

Let every harvest be a sign,
Of love that weaves through the divine.
In fields of hope, our spirits soar,
As we give thanks forevermore.

From Darkness to Holiness

In shadows deep, we search for light,
A flicker glows, dispelling night.
With every prayer, our spirits rise,
From darkness bleak to open skies.

Through trials faced and burdens bear,
We find the grace in whispered prayer.
Each stumble leads to paths of gold,
In faith's embrace, our hearts unfold.

Once lost in doubt, our eyes now see,
The guiding hand that sets us free.
In every tear, a lesson learned,
From darkness deep, our souls have turned.

Return to light, where hope ignites,
With holy love, we soar to heights.
In unity, our voices lift,
From sorrow's depths, we find our gift.

Together bound, in joy we tread,
The path of light, where angels led.
With hearts ablaze, we sing our song,
From darkness to the light, we belong.

Chants of the Reborn Earth

In cycles bright, the earth awakes,
From winter's grasp, new life it makes.
With every bloom, a sacred chant,
The song of life, where spirits dance.

The rivers flow, with purpose grand,
Throughout the land, they carve and brand.
In nature's heart, we find our place,
In harmony, the world we grace.

The trees provide their sheltering arms,
Their ancient wisdom, our spirit warms.
Chants of the wind, through leaves they weave,
In the quiet dusk, we believe.

From soil enriched, the flowers rise,
In colors bright, beneath the skies.
Every petal tells a tale of birth,
In whispered tones, the reborn earth.

So let us sing, with voices pure,
In reverence for the paths we endure.
Together we stand, in sacred mirth,
Embracing life on this blessed earth.

In Praise of a Gentle Breeze

A gentle breeze upon my face,
A whisper of the Divine's grace.
It dances lightly through the trees,
In every rustle, it carries pleas.

With every sigh, it stirs the soul,
A soothing balm that makes us whole.
The air we breathe, a sacred thread,
In every breath, where love is spread.

It carries scents of blooming flowers,
In tranquil hours, it softly empowers.
With kindness wrapped in nature's arms,
The gentle breeze displays its charms.

Through open fields and valleys wide,
It sweeps along, a faithful guide.
In gratitude, our hearts compose,
A hymn of joy, the spirit knows.

So let us pause, and feel its grace,
In every moment, in every place.
For in the breeze, we find our ease,
In praise of love, a gentle breeze.

Sacred Raindrops on Parched Ground

In the hush of desert night,
Hope descends, pure and bright.
Raindrops kiss the weary earth,
Bringing forth new life and mirth.

Grace flows in each gentle splash,
Filling hearts that longed to clash.
Nature sings a hymn so sweet,
As droplets dance on barren street.

From the heavens, blessings fall,
Answering the thirsty call.
The sun retreats, light dims the way,
Yet faith ignites, a bright array.

Crops awaken, roots embrace,
In every droplet, love and grace.
Faithful hands now work the land,
As sacred rain meets earthly sand.

Oh, miracle of life's return,
In parched ground, the spirits yearn.
With every storm, the promise found,
In sacred raindrops on parched ground.

Messengers of the Divine

Winds that whisper through the trees,
Carry blessings on the breeze.
Voices soft, yet clear they sing,
Of love and peace, eternal spring.

Stars that twinkle in the night,
Guide our hearts with gentle light.
Each a story, a path divine,
In their glow, our souls entwine.

Mountains rise to touch the sky,
Remind us we are never shy.
In their presence, strength we seek,
In humble hearts, the wise and meek.

Clouds that gather, storms that roar,
Breathe out truth from heaven's door.
In every trial, a lesson given,
A reminder of how to keep on livin'.

Messengers weave through the air,
In silence deep, they lay us bare.
With every moment, we receive,
The love that guides us, and believe.

In the Wake of Fury

Storms may rage and tempests cry,
Yet in their wake, we learn to fly.
Through shattered dreams, we find our way,
Beneath the dark, a brighter day.

Each tear that falls, a sacred sign,
A heart's lament, a soul's design.
From ashes rise, renewed and whole,
In fury's grasp, we seek our goal.

Lightning strikes but leaves a spark,
Illumining paths within the dark.
In chaos found, a strength reborn,
Where courage thrives, and hope is worn.

Yet in the fury, still we stand,
With faith and trust, united hand in hand.
Through every trial, we shall endure,
For love's embrace, it will be sure.

In the wake of storms once wild,
We become once more a child.
With hearts afire, we bravely tread,
On paths of grace, though fury led.

Dawn of Grace

As light breaks through the shadowed dawn,
New hope arises, fears are gone.
With gentle whispers, morning speaks,
A soft embrace, our spirit seeks.

Colors dance upon the sky,
Painting dreams that float nearby.
Each ray of sun, a warm caress,
In every heart, its sweet finesse.

The world awakens with a sigh,
As petals bloom and birds take flight.
In nature's choir, the praise begins,
For the grace that dwells within.

Clarity in every thought,
Lessons learned, wisdom sought.
The dawn unfolds, ripe and alive,
In every soul, the love will thrive.

So let us walk this sacred space,
Together bathed in dawn of grace.
For in each moment, we may find,
The beauty that unites mankind.

Echoes of the Past's Embrace

In shadows deep where whispers dwell,
The echoes of the night do swell.
Lessons learned through toil and prayer,
A sacred heart, a soul laid bare.

Time's tapestry weaves its thread,
In every word the ancients said.
Guided by faith, we find our way,
Through trials faced, we learn to pray.

The past, a voice that gently speaks,
In silence felt, its wisdom peaks.
Embracing all that's come before,
We rise anew from ancient lore.

With open hands, we hold the light,
To cherish love that banished night.
Each step we take, a step in grace,
With every tear, we find our place.

In every heartbeat, in every sigh,
The past remains, it will not die.
Through faith restored, we build anew,
United, strong, with hearts so true.

The Sacred Raindrop's Journey

A raindrop falls from heaven's grace,
It carries dreams, a soft embrace.
Through clouds it dances, crystal clear,
To quench the earth and calm our fear.

Each drop a prayer, each drop a sigh,
Connecting hearts, it drifts on high.
From sky to soil, a journey bold,
The sacred story, quietly told.

In gardens bloomed, in rivers wide,
The raindrop's touch, a loving guide.
It binds the world in gentle sway,
Renewing life with every spray.

When storms arise and shadows play,
Remember well the raindrop's way.
For in its path, the promise gleams,
A journey wrought from hopeful dreams.

So with each drop, let spirits rise,
To wash away our sorrowed cries.
In every fall, a blessing flows,
The sacred raindrop, love bestows.

Lifting the Veil of Woe

When darkness lingers, hearts are bound,
In silent tears, our burdens found.
Yet hope ignites in shadows deep,
Awakening dreams, the soul's to keep.

With whispered prayers, we seek the light,
A gentle touch dispels the night.
The veil of woe begins to fray,
As faith emerges, leading the way.

In every struggle, strength we find,
To cast aside our weary mind.
In unity, we stand as one,
Transforming pain, life's race begun.

Through trials faced, we learn to soar,
Reaching beyond what was before.
Each moment shared, a hand to hold,
Together rising, brave and bold.

In lifting veils, we claim the dawn,
With every sorrow, hope is drawn.
So in our hearts, let love ignite,
A beacon glimmers, pure and bright.

Breathed Anew

In stillness found, the breath of life,
Awakens hope amidst the strife.
With every inhale, spirits rise,
To greet the dawn with open eyes.

A sacred moment, gentle grace,
As whispers echo in this place.
Through trials faced, we learn to see,
With gratitude, we set us free.

The present blooms, a fragrant hue,
With every heartbeat, love shines through.
Embracing all, though scarred and bruised,
We find rebirth in sacred views.

So breathe in deep, let shadows part,
The universe sings within the heart.
In every breath, creation's song,
A journey shared where we belong.

Each moment granted, cherished, true,
In unity, we start anew.
For life's sweet breath is ours to claim,
In the dance of love, we find our name.

The Promise of the Rainbow

In storms of sorrow, a vow appears,
A ribbon of colors, calming our fears.
Heaven's embrace, a covenant bright,
Reminding us all of the coming light.

With each gentle arc, a story unfolds,
Of grace and mercy in hues of gold.
Nature's brush paints, the sky holds its breath,
A promise of hope, beyond shadow and death.

The raindrops weep, but their tears are few,
For in their falling, the sky finds its hue.
In every downfall, the joy will arise,
A testament shining from earth to the skies.

When life seems bleak, and doubt takes its claim,
The rainbow appears, igniting the flame.
With every bright color, a longing is sown,
In faith we find light, never stand alone.

So let us rejoice in the arcs that we see,
For hope is a flower that blooms endlessly.
Through storms we are guided, to visions profound,
In the promise of rainbows, our peace shall be found.

The Silence of the Heavens

In quiet repose, the stars softly gleam,
A tapestry woven from our every dream.
The universe whispers, its secrets unfold,
In stillness we find what can't be retold.

The moon hangs high, a sentinel's gaze,
Illuminating paths through life's winding maze.
With breath held in awe, we gaze at the night,
In the silence of heavens, our hearts take flight.

Each heartbeat a prayer, in the quiet we hear,
The murmurs of angels, tender and near.
The absence of sound, a sacred refrain,
Inviting our souls to break free from the chain.

With every dawn, the world starts anew,
Yet still, the vast cosmos holds fast to the few.
In the spaces between, where whispers come true,
The silence of heavens leads us right to You.

Let us embrace, in the calm of the night,
The wisdom of darkness, the grace of the light.
In stillness we bloom, as stars gently sway,
In the silence of heavens, our spirits will stay.

From Shadows to Light

In valleys of darkness, where fears tend to grow,
A flicker of warmth begins to bestow.
Through trials and shadows, we strive and we fight,
As hearts seek the path that leads from the night.

With courage we stand, though the journey be long,
Each step moves us closer, to the glimmer of song.
From ashes we rise, like a phoenix in flight,
Transcending the burdens that fade into light.

The dawn breaks anew, painting skies with its hue,
Illuminating dreams that once felt like a queue.
In the embrace of the morn, our worries take flight,
For hope's gentle presence turns shadows to light.

With faith as our guide, we walk hand in hand,
In the warmth of connection, together we stand.
Across fields of struggle, our spirits unite,
In the promise that love will banish the night.

So let us remember, when darkness unfolds,
That light is a promise, a truth to behold.
From shadows to brilliance, our souls take their flight,
In each fleeting moment, we chase after light.

The Spirit of Restoration

In brokenness lies the seeds of repair,
A gentle reminder that love's everywhere.
In chaos and storm, a still voice will call,
To heal every wound, and uplift us all.

Through trials we wander, in loss we may grieve,
Yet restoration blooms in what we believe.
With every loss, there's a chance to renew,
As dawn breaks the darkness with colors so true.

The valley may echo with sounds of despair,
Yet hope is a whisper that's waiting to share.
In shadows we gather, drawing close in our plight,
For together we shine, igniting the night.

In fragments of faith, our spirits combine,
Where sorrow once lingered, now courage will shine.
Through hands intertwined, and hearts that ignite,
The spirit of restoration brings forth the light.

So breathe in the beauty of mended souls,
For healing is woven in us, it consoles.
In the tapestry of life, every thread is a part,
The spirit of restoration flows deep in the heart.

The Lifting of Shadows

In the dawn, light breaks free,
Shadow's grasp, released like a plea.
Heaven's breath warms the heart,
Guiding souls, a new start.

Faith like a river flows wide,
Through valleys of doubt, we abide.
With each step, the darkness fades,
In grace, our spirit cascades.

Angels sing in quiet refrain,
Through trials, love conquers pain.
Beneath the veil, hope ignites,
In unity, our will unites.

The whispers of truth softly call,
In sacred halls, we stand tall.
Every tear, a seed that thrives,
In the light, our spirit strives.

Lifted high, our voices soar,
In worship, we seek evermore.
With open hearts, we embrace,
In His arms, we find our place.

Murmurs of the Sacred Grove

In the grove where silence reigns,
Whispers dance on ancient pains.
Leaves tremble with holy grace,
Nature's hymn, a soft embrace.

Each branch cradles the skies above,
Echoing tales of boundless love.
Forgotten paths, now walked anew,
Beneath the stars, hearts break through.

A brook babbles wisdom's lore,
In the stillness, we seek for more.
Nature's hands, both wild and kind,
In her arms, true peace we find.

The wind carries prayers like seeds,
In every gust, the soul concedes.
Roots entwined in sacred ground,
In this haven, grace is found.

Together in this timeless place,
We lift our eyes to seek His face.
Murmurs rise like smoke to the skies,
In every leaf, His spirit lies.

Resilience in Faith

Through storms that roar and winds that howl,
In darkest nights, we learn to prowl.
Resilient hearts, unbroken wings,
In trials faced, our spirit sings.

Each challenge met, a step we take,
With courage born from love's awake.
In shadows cast, we rise anew,
Embraced in grace, His light comes through.

With every tear, we plant the ground,
From sacred loss, new strength is found.
In faith's embrace, we stand as one,
Together forged, our race is run.

Mountains moved by prayerful might,
In whispered hopes, we ignite the light.
With hearts entwined, we face the night,
In resilience, we find our sight.

Through trials of life, we bear our truth,
With wisdom gleaned from everlasting youth.
Hand in hand, we rise above,
In faith unyielded, we find our love.

Restoring Eden's Whisper

In gardens lost, we seek to mend,
With holy hands, our hearts extend.
Beneath the skies, in gentle grace,
We restore joy in sacred place.

Harmony sings in colors bright,
In every bloom, a sacred light.
From ashes rise, a spirit pure,
Through love's embrace, we find the cure.

The rivers flow with stories old,
Of promises shared, and hope retold.
In each gesture, we plant a seed,
To heal this world with love's own creed.

As branches sway with timeless prayer,
We find our way, our burdens share.
With open hearts, we intercede,
In Eden lost, we plant the seed.

Together we walk, our spirits twined,
In nature's arms, peace we find.
Restoring whispers in the air,
In harmony, a holy prayer.

Healing in the Silence

In quiet places, peace is found,
Where whispers of the spirit abound.
Each breath a prayer, a gentle sigh,
Healing flows as we draw nigh.

In the midst of turmoil's roar,
A sacred calm opens the door.
In solitude, we find our guide,
With faith as our steadfast abide.

The heart unburdens, light we share,
In silence, we learn how to care.
Embracing love, we slowly mend,
In this stillness, we transcend.

Each moment births a sacred sound,
In silence, the lost are found.
Through trials, our spirits grow,
In the quiet, we learn to flow.

So let us gather, hand in hand,
In silence, together we stand.
Through the dark, hope shines bright,
Healing in the sacred light.

A Tapestry of Grace

Threads of mercy, woven tight,
In every shadow, there is light.
With every stitch, a tale unfolds,
A tapestry of grace, pure gold.

In the fabric of our lives,
Compassion blooms, love survives.
Every heart, a sacred loom,
Creating beauty from the gloom.

In laughter shared and tears that fall,
We find the strength to heed the call.
Together we rise, souls entwined,
In unity, our purpose defined.

From brokenness, new patterns grow,
In the garden of grace, seeds we sow.
Through trials faced, we learn to see,
The hand of God, lovingly free.

Each thread we weave with faith and care,
A masterpiece beyond compare.
In every heart, His love we trace,
Life's wonders, a tapestry of grace.

The Genesis of Tomorrow

In dawn's embrace, hope is reborn,
A canvas bright and newly worn.
With faith as our compass, we strive,
Embracing the dreams that come alive.

Each moment whispers, forward we go,
In the heart of the storm, love's light will glow.
With courage, we step on paths unknown,
Finding strength in the seeds we've sown.

A journey unfolds, divinely planned,
With every heartbeat, we take a stand.
Together we rise, united and strong,
A chorus of grace, our souls belong.

In the vastness of skies, visions take flight,
We weave our stories, stars shining bright.
With open hearts, we choose to believe,
Embracing the gifts each day can weave.

So let us gather, hand in hand,
In faith, together we stand.
For in this moment, hope will soar,
Genesis of tomorrow, opening the door.

Breaches of Light

In cracks of darkness, light breaks free,
A radiant truth for all to see.
Through sorrow's veil, hope shines through,
In every heart, a spark anew.

Each moment fragile, yet divine,
In healing hands, love intertwines.
With broken hearts, we find our voice,
Amidst the chaos, we rejoice.

Every tear that falls, a promise made,
In shadows cast, our fears will fade.
From wounds, we rise, a phoenix flight,
Renewed in faith, we chase the light.

In the distance, a beacon calls,
Embracing those who've faced the falls.
Together we stand in warmth and grace,
In breaches of light, we find our place.

So let us gather, souls embraced,
In love's warm glow, we are encased.
For in the darkness, our spirits ignite,
Breaches of light, a divine right.

Whispers of the Cleansed Earth

In the quiet of dawn's embrace,
Nature sighs, a gentle grace.
Birds take flight, a song in air,
Whispers of life, a sacred prayer.

Mountains stand, with crowns of snow,
Rivers flow in a holy glow.
Leaves rustle soft, in sacred dance,
Echoes of faith, in each glance.

The earth breathes deep, its canvas pure,
With every storm, it learns to endure.
In sacred soil, seeds of hope grow,
Life's tapestry, a vibrant show.

Hands that toil, with hearts aligned,
In unity, the lost shall find.
The cleansing rain, it falls divine,
Water of life, our souls entwine.

From ashes rise, the spirit's flame,
In each rebirth, we call His name.
Whispers echo, in harmony true,
Cleansed earth waits, for me and you.

The Breath of Renewal

From shadows deep, the light breaks free,
The breath of hope, our hearts decree.
In stillness found, the soul ascends,
A promise kept, as darkness ends.

Awakened dreams in silence stir,
The dawn of grace, in every blur.
Nature's hymns, in rhythm play,
The breath of renewal guides our way.

In gentle whispers, spirits rise,
The ancient path, beneath the skies.
With every breeze, the world does sing,
The joy of life, in everything.

Moments cherished, like grains of sand,
Together strong, we take our stand.
With faith as roots, we grow anew,
In the garden of love, pure and true.

Awake, arise, a call to all,
In love's embrace, we shall not fall.
The breath of life, in every heart,
A sacred bond that will not part.

Through Tempest's Veil

Beneath the storm, in dark of night,
We seek the spark, the flicker of light.
Through tempest's veil, our hearts remain,
In faith we stand, through loss and pain.

The thunder roars, yet still we sing,
In trials faced, our spirits cling.
With every wave, we learn to fight,
Through tempest's veil, we find our light.

A beacon shines, from distant shores,
Where hope abides, and spirit soars.
In the eye of storms, a calm retrieves,
Through tempest's veil, the heart believes.

Unified, we rise as one,
Each battle fought, till victory's won.
In darkest days, love's flame ignites,
Through tempest's veil, we claim our rights.

Hand in hand, we face the night,
With every step, we seek the light.
Through shadows deep, our voices rise,
In unity, a boundless prize.

Light Breaking on the Horizon

In the dawn's soft glow, grace unfolds,
Light breaking forth, a story told.
With every ray, our spirits lift,
A sacred moment, a holy gift.

Mountains tremble, in this glow,
As hope awakens, seeds we sow.
Through trials faced, the path seems clear,
Light breaking forth, our souls draw near.

The sun will rise, on weary hearts,
Hope redeems, and fear departs.
In every shadow, a promise gleams,
Light breaking forth, igniting dreams.

Together we walk, towards the dawn,
With faith unyielding, we carry on.
In every challenge, love prevails,
Light breaking forth, in whispered tales.

So let us venture, with hearts ablaze,
In the warmth of love, our spirits praise.
Light breaking forth, a guiding creed,
In the garden of life, we plant each seed.

Rays of Grace

In the hush of morning light,
Angels whisper soft and bright,
Guiding hearts to paths of love,
Sending peace from realms above.

Each step forms a holy dance,
Trusting in a sacred chance,
Faith unfolds like petals pure,
In His arms, we feel secure.

Hope ignites with every prayer,
Casting shadows from despair,
Grace descends like gentle rain,
Healing wounds, transforming pain.

With each moment, mercy flows,
Rays of light through pain and woes,
In the quiet, Spirit sings,
Life awakens with new wings.

In this journey, we embrace,
Every trial, a gift of grace,
Holding tight to love divine,
In the heart, the sun will shine.

Banners of Calm

In the stillness of the night,
Banners rise within our sight,
Spreading peace on winds of prayer,
As we seek what's truly fair.

Guided by the lantern's glow,
Pathways traced we do not know,
Yet we trust each step we take,
In the heart, our souls awake.

Whispers soft as morning dew,
Fill our spirits, pure and true,
Holding close what we believe,
In His love, we learn to cleave.

With each dawn, new strength we find,
In quiet moments, hearts entwined,
Through the trials, patience reigns,
In His arms, we break the chains.

Banners of calm, forever wave,
In the storm, we find the brave,
Every heartbeat, rhythmic song,
In His love, we all belong.

Traces of Heaven's Tears

When the skies begin to weep,
Traces of love our hearts will keep,
Sparkling drops of grace descend,
Washing sorrows, wounds will mend.

In every tear, a tale unfolds,
Stories shared of love retold,
Pouring forth from skies above,
Gentle echoes of His love.

Through the hurt and through the pain,
Healing comes like sweet refrain,
In His hands, we find our peace,
Every burden, sweet release.

Blessed are those who wash and weep,
For in sorrow, joy will creep,
Finding beauty in despair,
Carried forth on wings of prayer.

Traces linger deep within,
Reminding us we live again,
Through the storms, and through the fears,
We find solace in His tears.

A Pilgrimage to Serenity

On this road, we seek the light,
A pilgrimage through darkest night,
With each step, we breathe in grace,
Finding solace in His face.

Mountains high and valleys low,
In His love, we learn to grow,
Every heartbeat, sacred rite,
Guiding us toward the bright.

In the whispers of the trees,
Songs of joy upon the breeze,
Nature's voice, a gentle guide,
Leading hearts where dreams reside.

Through the trials, faith will bloom,
Filling hearts with sweet perfume,
In the journey, we evolve,
In His love, our fears dissolve.

A pilgrimage to find our peace,
In His arms, our spirits cease,
Every moment, heaven's grace,
We surrender, find our place.

The Renewal of Spirit

In silence I seek the sacred light,
A whispering grace that warms the night.
Each breath a prayer, a gentle plea,
To guide my heart and set it free.

Through trials faced, the spirit grows,
In love's embrace, true faith bestows.
Hope flourishes where shadows flowed,
A path of peace in grace is sowed.

The morning sun, with tender kiss,
Restores my soul to boundless bliss.
In every challenge, I will find,
A sacred purpose intertwined.

As rivers flow to oceans deep,
So too my heart in trust shall leap.
Embracing change, I rise anew,
In every ending, life's debut.

The spirit dances in the breeze,
With open arms, I bow and seize.
To cherish moments, small or grand,
In whispered hope, together we stand.

Blossoming Beneath the Heavens

In gardens green, where flowers bloom,
I feel Thy presence, dispelling gloom.
Each petal soft, a story told,
Of love divine, of faith so bold.

Beneath the sky, so vast and wide,
My spirit swells with love inside.
In every color, joy reveals,
The beauty in the heart that heals.

With every dawn, the world awakes,
A symphony that hope remakes.
Through trials faced, I stand my ground,
In nature's grace, my peace is found.

The starlit night, a canvas bright,
A tapestry of purest light.
In quiet moments, I can see,
The hand of God embracing me.

So let my soul bloom forth in song,
In every note, where I belong.
Together with the earth I'll tread,
In harmony, our spirits wed.

A Testament to the Tides

The ocean speaks in rhythmic flows,
A dance of power as nature knows.
Each wave that crashes, a sacred call,
To rise with faith and never fall.

In cycles turning, day to night,
The tides of life, a wondrous sight.
With every ebb, there comes a flow,
A journey bound, yet free to grow.

The moon above, a guiding light,
In shadows cast, it shines so bright.
Reflections deep, our truths reveal,
The endless love that we can feel.

Through storms that rage and calm that stays,
In nature's heart, our spirit plays.
To trust the course with open mind,
In each wave's crest, true peace we find.

With gratitude, I sing of tides,
In every swell, Your love abides.
A testament to life so grand,
Together, Lord, we form a band.

The Altar of the Cleansing Flood

In waters pure, we bow in trust,
A river flows where hearts combust.
With every drop, our sins are cast,
And hope restored, we breathe at last.

We gather here beneath the grace,
To seek anew this sacred space.
In cleansing waves, our spirits rise,
With faith as true as endless skies.

The altar waits for souls to mend,
Embracing all that God would send.
In silence deep, we find our plea,
A promise kept, forever free.

Upon this shore, we shed our doubt,
With fervent prayer, we sing out loud.
The cleansing flood, it purifies,
In this embrace, our spirit flies.

So let us wade in waters bright,
Revived by love, we seek the light.
For in this tide, our hearts unite,
As one we stand, our future bright.

Pillars of Peace Erected

Upon the stones of ancient grace,
We build our dreams in sacred space.
Pillars rise, strong and bold,
With whispers sweet, a truth retold.

In every heart, a quiet song,
Of hope that sings where we belong.
The light of peace, a guiding star,
In unity, we've come so far.

With hands embraced, we stand as one,
Creating bonds 'til day is done.
These pillars hold our faith in trust,
In every trial, we rise from dust.

May every soul that seeks to find,
A refuge warm, a love so kind.
Graced by the charge of higher calls,
We sow the seeds where spirit falls.

So let us rise, with hearts awake,
For in this peace, no bond shall break.
Together, we shall walk this way,
And greet the dawn of every day.

Miracles in the Mellowed Air

In whispered winds, where echoes play,
The gentle touch of God's own ray.
Miracles dance in softened light,
Guiding lost souls through darkest night.

With every breath, the heart beats strong,
In realms of hope, we all belong.
Each moment shines, a precious gift,
In love's embrace, our spirits lift.

The air is thick with sacred dreams,
Where faith abounds in flowing streams.
In every sigh, a prayer takes flight,
A tapestry of pure delight.

Together here, we weave the day,
In grace, we find our vibrant way.
For every tear that's softly shed,
A miracle blooms where hearts are fed.

So let us breathe in this sweet air,
With open hearts, we will declare.
In miracles, our lives shall thrive,
With gratitude, we come alive.

Beneath the Weathered Canopy

Beneath the leaves of ancient trees,
We gather close, our hearts at ease.
In nature's arms, a solace found,
Here, hope and love are tightly wound.

The weathered bark, a witness true,
To every prayer that's whispered through.
With branches high, and roots so deep,
Within this faith, we find our keep.

Each rustling leaf tells tales of old,
Of souls united, brave and bold.
As shadows play and sunlight beams,
We walk the path of shared dreams.

In sacred silence, we shall tread,
With every word, our spirits fed.
For under this vast canopy,
We find the strength to just be free.

So journey forth, beneath this dome,
In nature's heart, we find our home.
Together here, our love shall grow,
Beneath the trees, the world aglow.

The Refreshing Touch of the Divine

In the silence of dawn, whispers call,
Gentle breath of life, embracing all.
With open hearts, we seek the grace,
In love's warm light, we find our place.

Hands outstretched, we feel the flow,
From heavenly heights, blessings bestow.
Each tear we shed, a silver stream,
Washing away shadows, igniting our dream.

With every prayer, we rise anew,
In the sacred glow, the heart breaks through.
Revived by mercy, the soul does sing,
Finding comfort in the joys that He brings.

Mountains bow down, heavens align,
The universe hums, in rhythm divine.
Eternity whispers, "You are not alone,"
In the silence of faith, a love fully grown.

As night turns to dawn, we're reborn,
In the arms of grace, forever sworn.
Let us walk in purpose, with spirits aflame,
In the refreshing touch, we glorify His name.

Memoirs of a Renewed Soul

Once lost in shadows, now basking in light,
Awakening dreams that dance in the night.
Each moment a gift, each heartbeat a prayer,
In the book of my life, His love lays bare.

From ashes of sorrow, the phoenix will rise,
With wings of compassion, we soar to the skies.
Memories woven in threads of His grace,
In the tapestry bright, we find our place.

In whispers of twilight, my spirit takes flight,
Fueled by the hope that banishes night.
With each step I venture, my faith guides me through,
The memoirs I gather, all centered on You.

With love as my compass, I journey along,
In joy and in trial, I'll sing my song.
A renewed soul dancing to harmonies pure,
With every endeavor, in Him I'm secure.

Oh, the memories treasured, the moments I've shared,
An odyssey forged, with hearts that have dared.
In the light of His wisdom, I finally see,
The memoirs of grace that forever will be.

A Dance Beneath the Sun

In the warm embrace of the golden rays,
We celebrate life in luminous ways.
With hearts wide open, spirits set free,
A dance beneath the sun, just You and me.

Each twirl and each leap, a prayer in motion,
Beneath the vast sky, a soulful devotion.
The rhythm of nature, we sway with delight,
In the dance of creation, the world feels right.

With every step forward, the shadows retreat,
In the light of His love, we find our beat.
Each sunrise a promise, each sunset a sigh,
In the arms of the heavens, together we fly.

As petals unfold in a garden of dreams,
We gather the blessings like shimmering beams.
In laughter and joy, we cherish the run,
In our dance of gratitude, we are all one.

With the sun as our witness, we move as one heart,
In the dance of the spirit, we'll never part.
Forever united in this sacred day,
A dance beneath the sun, come what may.

Signs from the Celestial Sphere

Stars whisper secrets in the night sky,
Guiding lost souls as they soar and fly.
Cosmic melodies in celestial tune,
Each sign a promise, a love we attune.

From the depths of the void, a light does gleam,
Reflecting His grace in our waking dream.
With every heartbeat, we grasp the divine,
In the dance of the spheres, our spirits entwine.

The moon's gentle glow, a beacon of peace,
In the stillness of night, our worries shall cease.
Signs paint the heavens, stories unfold,
With whispers of hope, our hearts are consoled.

Through trials and triumphs, we're never astray,
In the vastness of space, love lights our way.
With each constellation, a truth we embrace,
In signs from the heavens, we cherish His grace.

In every moment, a lesson refined,
The signs that surround us, their messages bind.
With eyes turned upward, we seek and we strive,
In the signs from the sky, our spirits revive.

Grace in the Aftermath

In silence, we gather, hearts intertwined,
After the storm, our spirits aligned.
Through echoes of sorrow, whispers of grace,
We rise from the ashes, our fears we embrace.

Each tear that we shed, a prayer in the night,
Guiding our souls towards the light.
With faith as our anchor, we'll carry the load,
Together we journey, on this shared road.

The beauty of healing, a tapestry spun,
Threads of compassion, where hope has begun.
In moments of darkness, we find our way through,
With love as our lantern, we will pursue.

Grace flows like rivers, unending and pure,
Through valleys of doubt, our hearts will endure.
Each step that we take, a testament bright,
To the power of love, a beacon of light.

In unity's bond, we find our true strength,
A gathering of souls, in spirit and length.
Hand in hand we march, though shadows may loom,
For together we flourish, where hope will bloom.

Celestial Tears and Earthly Hope

The heavens weep softly, stars glimmer and glow,
Each tear from above, a promise bestowed.
In darkness, we seek what the heart understands,
The love that transcends time, uniting our hands.

Earth cradles our dreams beneath its great sky,
As whispers of hope in the night dare to fly.
With faith as our armor, we silently stand,
Embracing our purpose, united and grand.

Clouds part for a moment, revealing the dawn,
A vision of grace, where sorrow is gone.
In trials, we forge bonds, unbreakable, true,
With each fleeting moment, our spirits renew.

Amidst the great chaos, a symphony swells,
With melodies woven from heart's hidden wells.
Where love meets the weary, we gather our might,
In celestial tears, we find our own light.

In harmony's whispers, we find our release,
As life ebbs and flows, we embrace the peace.
With earthly hope guiding, we wander and roam,
In the arms of the heavens, we find our true home.

A Covenant of Winds

In the dance of the breezes, whispers unite,
A covenant woven, in shadows and light.
Each gust a reminder, of promises bound,
In the breath of creation, grace can be found.

The winds tell the stories of ages gone by,
Echoing wisdom, where dreams learn to fly.
In the rustle of leaves, we gather our prayer,
With each whispered promise, we find solace there.

Through valleys and mountains, the currents do flow,
Carrying secrets where only hearts know.
In unity spoken, we weather the storm,
With hope in our souls, a new world to form.

As dawn kisses twilight, the cycle renews,
With courage, we rise, embracing the hues.
In the spirit of winds, we are never alone,
For together, we journey toward the unknown.

Each gust is a promise, a sacred refrain,
As we walk through the shadows, through joy and through pain.
Embracing the whispers, and trusting the flow,
In a covenant of winds, together we grow.

Resilience Forged in Turmoil

Amidst the raging storm, our souls stand tall,
In trials we gather, answering the call.
Each struggle a lesson, etched deep in our core,
In the fires of turmoil, our spirits will soar.

With hands intertwined, we navigate fears,
Finding strength in our voices, through laughter and tears.

In the darkness, we sing, a song of release,
For in facing the tempest, we find our true peace.

The weight of our burdens, if shared, becomes light,
In community's embrace, we turn darkness to light.
With courage as compass, we dare to believe,
In the power of stories that help us achieve.

From the wreckage of yesterday, we rise ever strong,
With hope in our hearts, we're where we belong.
Through the echoes of struggle, our voices will ring,
In resilience, we flourish, in unity, we sing.

The path may be winding, but together we stand,
Our spirits unbroken, we walk hand in hand.
For within every storm lies a glimpse of the dawn,
Resilience, our shield, our true light reborn.

A Reflection in Still Waters

In the mirror of the lake, so clear,
Whispers of angels come to near.
Each rippling wave a prayer we send,
Beneath the sky, our souls ascend.

The sun dips low, a golden hue,
Light dances softly, pure and true.
In quiet moments, grace abounds,
In stillness, lost is where we're found.

Nature's hymn, a sacred song,
In every breeze, we feel we belong.
Reflecting on the love we share,
In every heartbeat, everywhere.

O Lord, in waters calm and deep,
Your promises, like dreams, we keep.
With humble hearts, we seek your face,
In still waters, we find your grace.

A tapestry of faith is spun,
In stars above, your will be done.
With every echo of the night,
We find our peace, and hearts take flight.

The Lament of the Winds

Whispers of sorrow through the trees,
A symphony carried by the breeze.
Each gust a story, oft untold,
In restless hearts, the truth unfolds.

Beneath the sky, the shadows play,
The winds lament in a mournful sway.
They sing of loss, of hopes once bright,
In twilight's grip, they seek the light.

Yet in their cries, a promise lies,
From every tear, new strength will rise.
For in each note, the soul can mend,
Through fear and doubt, our spirits blend.

Let not the storms our hearts confine,
In tempest's roar, your love will shine.
With every breeze, you guide our way,
Through darkest nights to brightest days.

So let the winds their stories share,
In every whisper, we find your care.
A dance of faith, a sacred vow,
In winds of change, we rest in you now.

Sanctuary Found

In the hush of dawn, the spirit calls,
Within the heart, true peace befalls.
A sacred space where shadows cease,
In quiet corners, there's sweet release.

Where ancient trees spread arms so wide,
In nature's arms, we can confide.
With every leaf, a prayer takes flight,
In gentle winds, our hopes ignite.

A sacred temple, built of grace,
In silence, find your holy place.
Through every sigh, through every breath,
In love's embrace, we conquer death.

In moments still, we seek your face,
In every heart, you leave a trace.
With open arms, we come undone,
In sanctuary, we are one.

Beneath the stars, our spirits soar,
In love's embrace, we ask for more.
Together united, we stand strong,
In sanctuary found, we belong.

The Quiet Unfolds

In the silence, all is revealed,
The quiet whispers, wounds are healed.
In gentle tones, the heart will sway,
In stillness, find the light of day.

With every breath, the world slows down,
In tranquil grace, wear peace as crown.
In sacred hush, our spirits rise,
Guided by love that never dies.

The subtle touch of heaven's grace,
In quiet moments, we find our place.
Within the stillness, courage grows,
A gentle breeze in us bestows.

In whispered prayers, our souls align,
In every heartbeat, your love shines.
Beneath the weight of worldly call,
In quiet unfold, we find it all.

In every pause, we hear the song,
A melody where we belong.
Wrapped in silence, strong and bold,
In the quiet, the truth unfolds.

The Rebirth of Serenity

In silence deep, the heart does dwell,
Awakening whispers from sacred well.
With each soft breath, the spirit soars,
Rebirth unfolds, as peace restores.

The dawn breaks forth, in golden hue,
A canvas bright, the skies anew.
Within the soul, a tranquil stream,
Flowing gently, love's sweet dream.

In nature's arms, we find our rest,
With humble grace, the world is blessed.
Every moment, a chance to grow,
In life's embrace, we learn to glow.

Through trials faced, we find our way,
In every tear, a chance to pray.
In forgiveness found, the burden light,
The rebirth of serenity, our guiding light.

So walk with faith, in paths of grace,
With open hearts, we seek His face.
In unity, our voices sing,
Of peace and love, true offering.

Raised Voices in Praise

With hands uplifted, we gather here,
Voices united, free of fear.
In joyous hymn, we lift our song,
To Him who guides us, ever strong.

In every heart, a flame ignites,
Shining bright through darkest nights.
Together we stand, in love's embrace,
Each note a prayer, a sacred space.

We chant the words, of ancient lore,
With every breath, our spirits soar.
In harmony, our souls entwine,
Transcending time, in love divine.

Oh, blessed unity, our souls proclaim,
In every song, we share His name.
With raised voices, our praises rise,
Forever singing 'neath open skies.

In gratitude, our hearts align,
For every blessing, His love benign.
Together, we stand, as one in grace,
Raised voices in praise, our sacred place.

A Garden Yet to Blossom

In the soil of faith, we plant the seed,
Watered by hope, and love's pure creed.
With tender care, the roots take hold,
A promise blooming, as tales unfold.

Amongst the thorns, we find our path,
In trials faced, we feel love's wrath.
Yet patience brings, the sweetest bloom,
In waiting's grace, dispelling gloom.

Sunlight kisses, the leaves that sway,
In gentle whispers, we find our way.
A garden growing, with every hour,
In faith we trust, for love's great power.

Though seasons change, and storms arise,
The garden breathes under open skies.
In every petal, a story lies,
A garden yet to blossom, reaches high.

With every dawn, new life awakes,
In heart and soul, our courage takes.
For through the struggle, beauty finds,
A garden yet to blossom, love binds.

Glimmers of Sacred Light

From shadows deep, the light will break,
A gentle touch, our hearts awake.
In every corner, traces found,
Of sacred love, profound and sound.

With every step upon this way,
We seek the truth, we long to stay.
In glimmers bright, our path is clear,
Guided by faith, we have no fear.

In whispers soft, His voice we hear,
Encouraging hearts to draw Him near.
Among the stars, His light does shine,
A promise whispered, forever divine.

Through trials faced, we hold heads high,
With glimmers of hope, we touch the sky.
In every tear, redemption flows,
A sacred journey, where love bestows.

In gratitude, we raise our hearts,
For every blessing, love imparts.
In glimmers of sacred light, we see,
The love that binds us, eternally.

Milton Keynes UK
Ingram Content Group UK Ltd.
UKHW021913201124
451474UK00013B/722